DK READERS

Level 1

Animal Hide and Seek
Animals at Home
A Bed for the Winter
Big Machines
Born to be a Butterfly
Bugs and Us
Busy Buzzy Bee
A Day at Greenhill Farm
A Day in the Life of a Builder
A Day in the Life of a Firefighter
A Day in the Life of a Police Officer
A Day in the Life of a Teacher
Dinosaur's Day
Diving Dolphin
Duckling Days
Feeding Time
First Day at Gymnastics
Homes Around the World
I Want to Be a Ballerina
Let's Play Soccer
Rockets and Spaceships
Submarines and Submersibles
Surprise Puppy!

Tale of a Tadpole
Train Travel
A Trip to the Dentist
A Trip to the Zoo
Truck Trouble
Whatever the Weather
Wild Baby Animals
Angry Birds Star Wars: Yoda Bird's Heroes
Indiana Jones: Indy's Adventures
John Deere: Good Morning, Farm!
LEGO® DC Super Heroes: Ready for Action!
LEGO® DUPLO: Around Town
LEGO® Pirates: Brickbeard's Treasure
Star Wars The Clone Wars: Ahsoka in Action
Star Wars The Clone Wars: Pirates . . . and Worse!
Star Wars The Clone Wars: Watch Out for Jabba the Hutt!
Star Wars: Luke Skywalker's Amazing Story
Star Wars: Ready, Set, Podrace!
Star Wars: Tatooine Adventures
Star Wars: What is a Wookiee?
Star Wars: Who Saved the Galaxy?

Level 2

Amazing Buildings
Animal Hospital
Astronaut: Living in Space
Boys' Life: Dinosaur Battles
Boys' Life: Tracking
Bugs! Bugs! Bugs!
Dinosaur Dinners
Earth Smart: How to Take Care of the Environment
Emperor Penguins
Eruption! The Story of Volcanoes
Fire Fighter!
The Great Migration
Horse Show
I Want to Be a Gymnast
Journey of a Humpback Whale
Let's Go Riding
The Little Ballerina
The Secret Life of Trees
Slinky, Scaly Snakes!
Sniffles, Sneezes, Hiccups, and Coughs
Starry Sky
The Story of Columbus
The Story of Pocahontas
Survivors: The Night the Titanic Sank
Twisters!
Water Everywhere
Winking, Blinking, Wiggling, and Waggling

Angry Birds Star Wars: Lard Vader's Villains
Angry Birds Star Wars: Path to the Pork Side
Indiana Jones: Traps and Snares
LEGO® DC Super Heroes: Super-Villains
LEGO® Friends: Let's Go Riding
LEGO® Hero Factory: Brain Attack
LEGO® Hero Factory: Meet the Heroes
LEGO® Kingdoms: Defend the Castle
LEGO® Legends of Chima: Tribes of Chima
LEGO® Monster Fighters: Meet the Monsters
LEGO® *Star Wars*: Attack of the Clones
LEGO® *Star Wars*: The Phantom Menace
Star Wars The Clone Wars: Anakin in Action!
Star Wars The Clone Wars: Boba Fett: Jedi Hunter
Star Wars The Clone Wars: Chewbacca and the Wookiee Warriors
Star Wars The Clone Wars: Jedi in Training
Star Wars The Clone Wars: Stand Aside— Bounty Hunters!
Star Wars: A Queen's Diary
Star Wars: Bounty Hunters for Hire
Star Wars: Clone Troopers in Action
Star Wars: Join the Rebels
Star Wars: Journey through Space
Star Wars: R2-D2 and Friends
Star Wars: The Adventures of Han Solo
X-Men: Meet the X-Men

A Note to Parents

DK READERS is a compelling program for beginning readers, designed in conjunction with leading literacy experts, including Dr. Linda Gambrell, Distinguished Professor of Education at Clemson University. Dr. Gambrell has served as President of the National Reading Conference, the College Reading Association, and the International Reading Association.

Beautiful illustrations and superb full-color photographs combine with engaging, easy-to-read stories to offer a fresh approach to each subject in the series. Each DK READER is guaranteed to capture a child's interest while developing his or her reading skills, general knowledge, and love of reading.

The five levels of DK READERS are aimed at different reading abilities, enabling you to choose the books that are exactly right for your child:

Pre-level 1: Learning to read
Level 1: Beginning to read
Level 2: Beginning to read alone
Level 3: Reading alone
Level 4: Proficient readers

The "normal" age at which a child begins to read can be anywhere from three to eight years old. Adult participation through the lower levels is very helpful for providing encouragement, discussing storylines, and sounding out unfamiliar words.

No matter which level you select, you can be sure that you are helping your child learn to read, then read to learn!

LONDON, NEW YORK, MUNICH,
MELBOURNE, and DELHI

Editorial Assistant Ruth Amos
Senior Editor Hannah Dolan
Designer Richard Horsford
Jacket Designer Rhys Thomas
Pre-Production Producer Rebecca Fallowfield
Producer Danielle Smith
Managing Editor Laura Gilbert
Design Manager Maxine Pedliham
Art Director Ron Stobbart
Publishing Manager Julie Ferris
Publishing Director Simon Beecroft
Reading Consultant
Linda B. Gambrell, Ph.D.
Lucasfilm
Executive Editor J. W. Rinzler
Art Director Troy Alders
Keeper of the Holocron Leland Chee
Director of Publishing Carol Roeder
Rovio
Approvals Editor Nita Ukkonen
Senior Graphic Designer Jan Schulte-Tigges
Publishing and Licensing Manager
Laura Nevanlinna
Vice President of Book Publishing
Sanna Lukander

First published in the United States in 2013 by
DK Publishing
345 Hudson Street, New York, New York 10014
10 9 8 7 6 5 4 3 2 1
001–196556–Nov/13

DK books are available at special discounts when purchased in bulk
for sales promotions, premiums, fund-raising, or educational use.
For details, contact:
DK Publishing Special Markets,
345 Hudson Street, New York, New York 10014
SpecialSales@dk.com

A catalog record for this book is available
from the Library of Congress.

ISBN: 978-1-4654-1537-0 (Paperback)
ISBN: 978-1-4654-1538-7 (Hardcover)

Color reproduction by Altaimage, UK
Printed and bound in China by L-Rex

Discover more at
www.dk.com
www.starwars.com

Contents

DK READERS

BEGINNING
1
TO READ

ANGRY BIRDS STAR WARS II

DARTH SWINDLE'S SECRETS

Written by Scarlett O'Hara

Criminal mastermind

Who is that hiding under
a hood?

It is the evil Pig Lord
Darth Swindle!

He has lots of nasty secrets.

Evil
grin

Hidden weapon

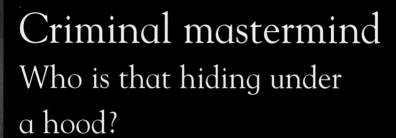

Swindle wants
to rule the
galaxy and eat
all the candy
and junk food.

His snout is
good for smelling
out food.

snout

The Pork Side

A lot of pigs are on sneaky
Swindle's side.
It is called the Pork Side.

Count Dodo

Copypig

Darth
Swindle

Battle pig

The pigs want to eat all
the junk food!
They also want to find The
Egg, which has the power
to rule the galaxy.

Warhog
Darth Moar

General
Grunter

Brave birds

Here are the good birds!
Some of the birds
are Jedi Bird warriors.
They are brave fighters.

C–3PYOLK

Moa Windu

Obi-Wan
Kaboomi

Quail-Gon

Only Yoda Bird knows where
to find The Egg.
It is disguised as R2-EGG2.
Don't tell Darth Swindle!

R2-EGG2

Queen Peckmé

Redkin
Skywalker

Jar Jar
Wings

Yoda Bird

Copypigs

Watch out! Darth Swindle
has an army of Copypigs.
He orders them to search the
galaxy for candy.

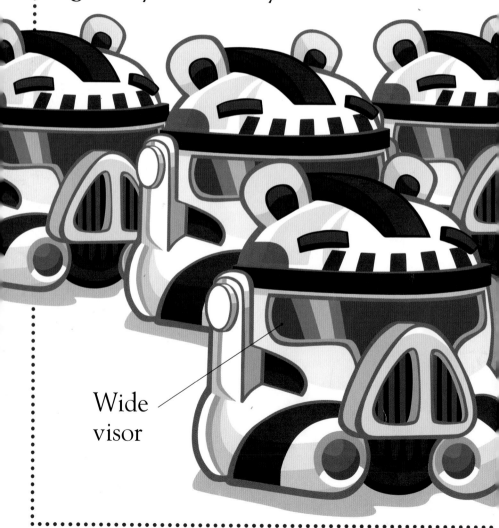

Wide
visor

The Copypigs are very stupid.
They do not understand
Swindle's greedy orders.
They copy one another
and get confused!

Piggy
ears

Sleek
gray hair

Snooty
face

Pig Lords

Darth Swindle commands
several pesky Pig Lords.

Count Dodo used to be a Jedi.
Now he is a horrible hog!

Fierce General Grunter's
body is made out of metal.
He fights with four lightsabers!

Lightsaber

Tough armor

Grunter's gang

General Grunter leads an army of droids.

Battle pigs are not very bright because their programming went wrong!

droids

Long snout

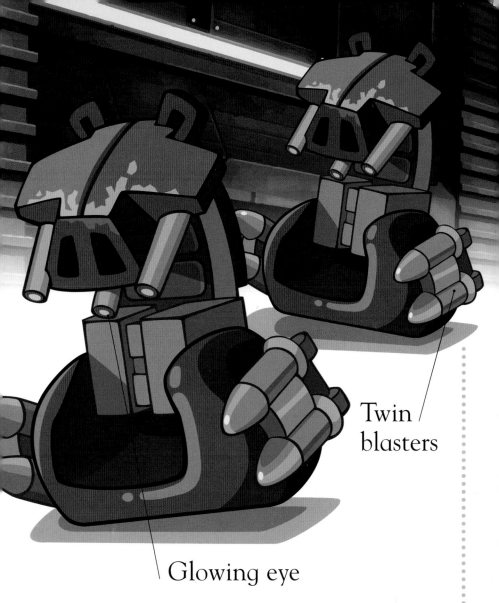

Twin
blasters

Glowing eye

The Warhogs are very fast and
have lots of weapons.
Everybody is scared of
them—even the Jedi Birds.

Frightened fowl

Goofy Jar Jar Wings
and loyal Terebacca
are in big trouble!

Furry feathers

Tough
metal shell

Eyes on
stalks

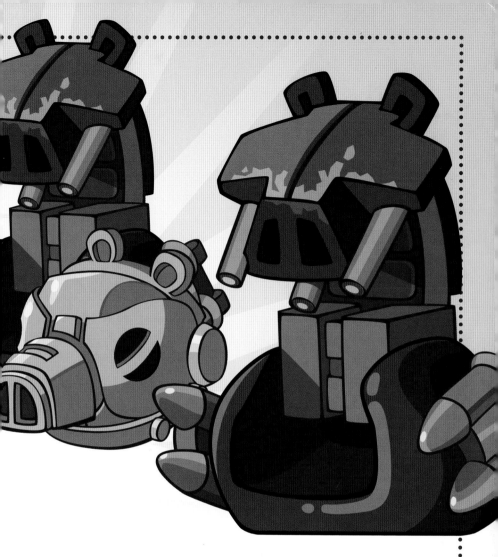

Darth Swindle thinks they
have hidden food from him.

Swindle sends in his droids
to teach them a lesson.

Jedi enemies

Darth Swindle has many enemies.

One enemy is the Jedi Bird Moa Windu.

Glowing lightsaber

Bushy brow

Moa is a great lightsaber fighter.

The wise Jedi Yoda Bird
and Moa talk together.
How can they stop Swindle?

Wise wrinkled
forehead

Dark pig power

Darth Swindle challenges
Moa to a duel.
Sly Swindle wants to defeat
Moa and rule the roost!

Pow! Swindle
zaps Moa with his
Force lightning.

Force
lightning

The wicked pig wins the fight.

Jedi cloak

Bounty hunters

Darth Swindle sends these bounty hunters to capture enemy birds.

Zam Weasel uses electro-goggles to find her target.

Zam's electro-goggles

electro-
goggles

Cunning Jango
Fatt uses a
jetpack to escape
from trouble.

Jango's jetpack

Crazy warrior

Watch out for this crazy pig!
His name is Darth Moar.

He is Darth Swindle's
pig apprentice.

Head
horn

Evil
grin

Moar joined the Pork Side when he was young.

Swindle tempted him with lots of junk food.

Staring eyes

Moar's mission

Darth Swindle sends his
apprentice on missions.

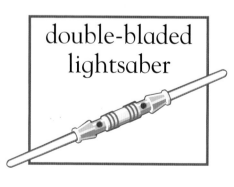

double-bladed
lightsaber

Moar has a
double-bladed
lightsaber.

Look! Darth Moar is trying
to capture Queen Peckmé.

Quail-Gon and Obi-Wan
try to stop him.

Powerful
blade

Green bird
lightsaber

Sharp beak

Battle scar

Tempting trick

Darth Swindle is
a very sly pig.
He tries to tempt
Jedi Birds over to
the Pork Side.

Swindle tempts Redkin
Skywalker to join the pigs.

Redkin becomes the Pig
Lord Lard Vader.

Huge
helmet

Watch out for the birds!

These birds won't let
Darth Swindle win.
They will fight back.

They will work together
to beat the evil Pork Side.
They will stop the pigs from
finding The Egg...

Glossary

Double-bladed lightsaber
A weapon with a beam of energy at each end.

Droids
A type of robot, like battle pigs or Warhogs.

Electro-goggles
Goggles used to spy on a person or thing.

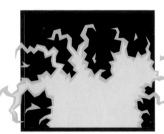

Force lightning
A deadly power that only Pig Lords use.

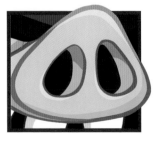

Snout
A round, flat nose that some animals have.

Index